Excel 2024
Pivot Tables

EASY EXCEL 2024 ESSENTIALS - BOOK 4

M.L. HUMPHREY

SELECT TITLES BY M.L. HUMPHREY

EXCEL 2024 ESSENTIALS
Excel 2024 for Beginners
Intermediate Excel 2024
Excel 2024 Useful Functions

EASY EXCEL 2024 ESSENTIALS
Formatting
Conditional Formatting
Charts
Pivot Tables
Newer Functions

See mlhumphrey.com for Microsoft Word, PowerPoint and Access titles and more

CONTENTS

Introduction

This book is part of the *Easy Excel 2024 Essentials* series of titles. These are targeted titles that are excerpted from the main *Excel 2024 Essentials* series and are focused on one specific topic.

If you want a more general introduction to Excel, then you should check out the *Excel 2024 Essentials* titles instead; in this case, *Intermediate Excel 2024* which covers pivot tables as well as a number of other topics, including charts and conditional formatting.

But if all you want is a book that covers this specific topic, then let's continue with a discussion of how to create and format pivot tables, including how to work with Slicers and Timelines.

Pivot Tables - Basics

I wrote the first ever Excel Essentials series just so I could teach writers how to use pivot tables, that's how valuable I think they are.

At their most basic, pivot tables (technically spelled PivotTables by the Office folks) are a quick and easy way to take a big table of data and summarize it. You don't have to worry about how things are sorted or which order your columns are in or writing the correct formula, you can just throw it all in a pivot table and Excel will do the hard work for you.

But there is a lot to know to use them effectively.

Now. A few things to keep in mind:

Pre-Prep

You may need to do a little work with your data first to clean it up and standardize it. For example, Excel can't tell that CO and Colorado are the same thing, so will treat them as different values. You'll want to take a copy of your data and fix issues like that before you start using a pivot table to summarize your results.

You should also make sure that your columns are formatted properly so that numbers are seen by Excel as numbers and dates are seen as dates. (See the quick tips chapter for how to fix dates when working with pivot tables.)

Also, remove any subtotals or grand totals, and make sure that each column of your data has a header in the first row of the table. (For me, I prefer that this is also the first row of the worksheet.)

And make sure that each row of data is complete in and of itself. You want to be working with a table of data not data formatted as a report.

Dynamic Nature

Also, be careful where you choose to build a pivot table. Pivot tables are dynamic. The amount of space they take up varies depending on your data and the choices you make about what to include in the table.

If you put a pivot table in a worksheet that has other information, you run a risk that the pivot table will overwrite that other data.

Pivot tables build to the right and down, so if you do put a pivot table in a worksheet that has other information in it, always add that pivot table to the right of and/or below your existing information.

And if you are ever tempted to add notes around an existing pivot table (like I sometimes do), understand that if you update the table you could either accidentally delete your notes, or the data in your pivot table could move so that it no longer matches up with your notes.

(This is one reason why if you use a formula and try to reference values in a pivot table it looks so weird. Excel can't just reference a cell like with normal data entries, it has to instead reference how the value in that cell was built.)

Okay. Now that we've gotten through the preliminaries, let's build one.

Insert

Assuming your header row is in the first row of your worksheet, select the columns that have your data, or use Select All. If your data table doesn't start at the top of the worksheet, then select all of the cells in your table, being sure to include the header row.

Next, go to the Tables section of the Insert tab, and click on the PivotTable image.

If you accidentally click on the dropdown arrow, the option you want is From Table/Range. (For the level of expertise I expect you to have if you're reading this book, I really do not recommend working with data in another workbook or from another source. It's too easy to break the link between your workbook and that external data source, so we're not going to go there.)

You should now see a PivotTable From Table or Range dialogue box:

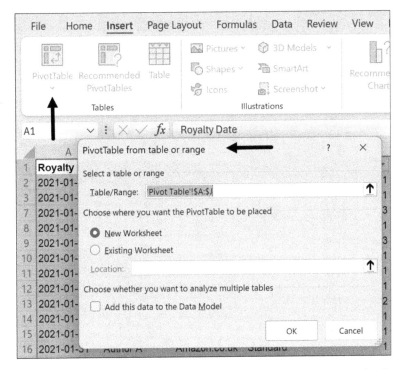

Usually, I just click OK here, because I already selected my data range, I don't work with data models, and I am fine with putting my pivot table in a new worksheet.

However, sometimes I do click on the option for Existing Worksheet instead, and then click somewhere to the right of the data in my current worksheet, to keep the data and the pivot table together in that same worksheet. I usually do that in workbooks where I have a lot of pivot tables I'm going to build to make sure I know the source of the data in each table.

At this point, you may see an error message if any of the cells in the first row of your selected data are blank. That's because Excel needs there to be something to label each column of data with.

If that happens, close out, and either add labels to the blank cells in the first row of your selected cell range, or delete any blank columns in your cell range.

If a blank column header isn't the issue, then you may need to fix your referenced cell range to make sure you captured the header row. Once you've fixed whatever the issue is, go through the above steps again.

By default, Excel will insert your pivot table starting in Cell A3 of a new worksheet:

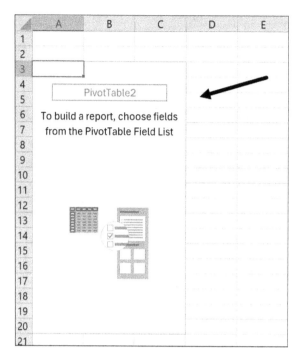

There won't be an actual pivot table there, though, until you tell Excel which fields to use. It just shows you that it's ready to put a pivot table there.

You should also see a PivotTable Fields task pane on the right-hand side of the workspace, as well as two new menu tabs, PivotTable Analyze and Design:

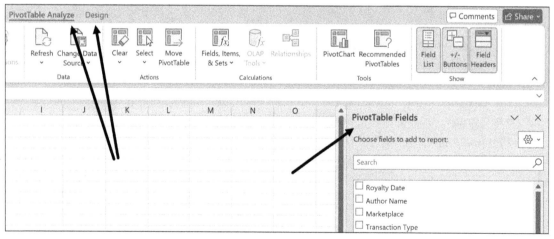

The task pane and tabs will be visible by default any time you're clicked onto a pivot table, but will go away when you click elsewhere in your worksheet or workbook. So to get them back if they ever disappear, just click onto your pivot table.

Build

The way you build a pivot table is by using the PivotTable Fields task pane on the right-hand side of the workspace.

Here is the full task pane:

The top section shows all of your available fields. At the start, that will be the names for each column of data you included. (Later it might include extra date-related fields or formulas if you add any.)

The bottom section has four parts: Filters, Columns, Rows, and Values. This is where you put each field to build the table.

The fields you place in Columns and/or Rows will provide the data labels you'll have either across the top (columns) or down the side (rows) of the table. Values is where you put the field(s) you're going to use for calculations.

Filters is for fields you aren't going to use in your columns, rows, or values sections, that you still want to use to narrow down the information displayed in the pivot table.

Let's walk through some examples to see how this works. We're going to use the same data I've been using throughout these books, which contains about six hundred lines of book sales data that includes fields for date of sale, author name, marketplace, type of transaction, number of units sold, currency, royalty, and converted royalty.

First, let's build a table that shows units sold for each author.

My Values field, what I want to use for my calculation, is going to be Units Sold. And then either my Row or Column field needs to be Author Name.

To do this, I simply left-click and drag each of those fields from the top of the PivotTable Fields task pane down to the appropriate section in the bottom of the task pane. I went with the Row section for Author Name because it looked better to me:

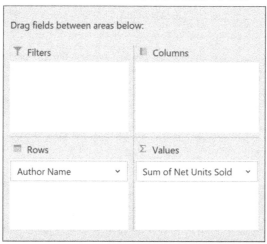

Another option for adding a field to a section, is to right-click on the field name in the top section, and then choose where to place the field from the dropdown menu:

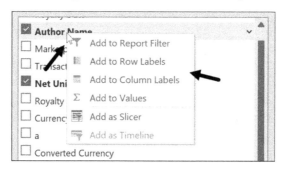

Either way works.

(In older versions of Excel you could also drag the field to the table in the worksheet, but that's no longer available by default. This is why it's always good to know at least two ways to do things in Excel. That way if they change one of the two, you can still use the other method.)

Okay.

Here is the pivot table that created:

	A	B	C
1			
2			
3	Row Labels ⌄	Sum of Net Units Sold	
4	Author C	90	
5	Author E	4	
6	Author B	20	
7	Author A	1242	
8	Author D	80	
9	Author F	3	
10	Author G	1	
11	(blank)		
12	**Grand Total**	**1440**	
13			

Excel automatically built the table as I placed each field.

Now let's make this more complex and add in Marketplace. I want to see how many units each author sold in each marketplace.

I also want to be able to see total sales by marketplace and total sales by author, which means one has to be in the Rows section and one has to be in the Columns section, they can't be together.

Because it was easy, I added Marketplace into the Columns section:

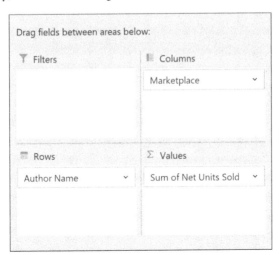

This is what that pivot table looks like:

	Amazon.ca	Amazon.co.uk	Amazon.com	Amazon.com.au	Amazon.com.mx	Amazon.de	Amazon.es	Amazon.fr	Amazon.in	Amazon.it	(blank)	Grand Total
Author A	15	90	1129	3	1		1	1		2		1242
Author B		10	7	3								20
Author C	3	1	81			3		1	1			90
Author D		3	76	1								80
Author E			3							1		4
Author F			3									3
Author G		1										1
(blank)												
Grand Total	18	105	1299	7	1	3	1	2	1	3		1440

Sum of Net Units Sold / Column Labels / Row Labels

I can easily see how many units each author sold in each marketplace, as well as totals for each author and totals for each marketplace.

Not bad for clicking and dragging three field names into place, huh?

Filter Pivot Table Data

Now let's apply a filter. To do that, add the field you want to use as your filter to the Filters area of the PivotTable Fields task pane.

For this example, I used Transaction Type:

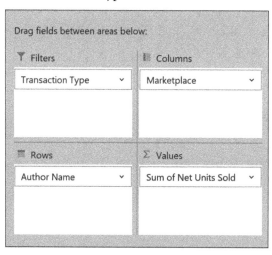

Doing that adds a dropdown menu above the pivot table that you can then use to change what information is displayed in the pivot table itself.

Here, for example, I limited the results to Free-Price Match. Now the pivot table only shows results for transactions that were free price match transactions:

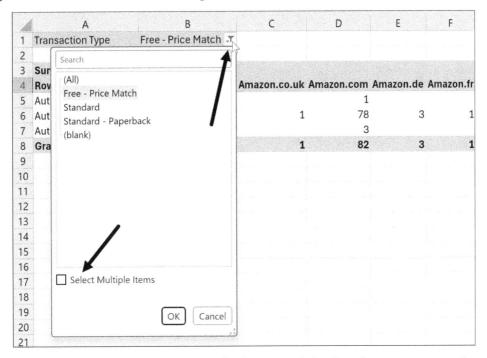

The filter dropdown works just like when you filter columns in a normal worksheet.

Click on the dropdown arrow or funnel on the right-hand edge of the cell (see below) that displays the current filter to see the dropdown.

Check the box for Select Multiple Items at the bottom of the dropdown so you can then check and uncheck the boxes to select the values you want to filter by. The default is All, so if you only want one or two values, uncheck that box for All to unselect all values first, and then check the ones you want.

You can also use the search field to narrow your results.

When you select a single value to filter by, like I did above, Excel will show that value, as you can see in Cell B1 of the pivot table we just built.

If you use multiple criteria, though, it will just say Multiple Items instead. In a situation like that, it may be better to use a Slicer, which is discussed in the next chapter.

Filter Values in Rows or Columns

There will be times when you want to use a field for your rows or columns sections, but you also want to limit which of those values display in the pivot table. You can't put that field in the Filters section, because you're using it in the Rows or Columns section already, and Excel won't let you do both.

Fortunately, you can still filter those values. Just click on the arrow next to Row Labels or Column Labels in your pivot table to bring up a filter dropdown menu for that field:

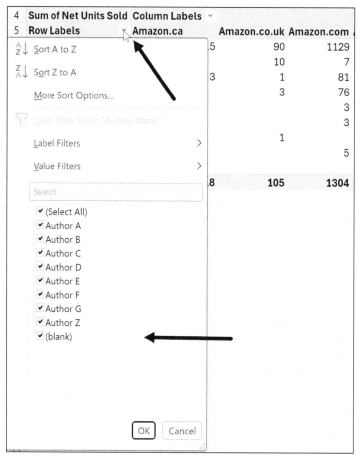

At that point it's just working with filters again.

If you have multiple fields in your rows or columns sections and want to filter on one of them, click on one of the values in the table for that field first, and *then* click on the arrow next to Row Labels or Column Labels.

Multiple Fields in a Section

You can use multiple fields in the Columns, Rows, Filters, and/or Values sections. To have multiple levels, just drag more than one field to that section.

For Columns and Rows, order matters. It's like with sorting. Put the field you want to be primary on top, and list secondary, tertiary, etc. fields below that in order of priority. Values for the primary field will only show up once. Values for the other fields can repeat.

Here, for example, I have a pivot table with Transaction Type in the first position and Author Name listed second:

4		⊞ Amazon.in
6	Free - Price Match	
7	Author C	1
8	Author F	
9	Author B	
10	Standard	
11	Author A	
12	Author D	
13	Author B	
14	Author C	
15	Author E	
16	Author G	
17	Standard - Paperback	
18	Author A	
19	Author D	
20	Author E	
21	Author B	
22	**Grand Total**	**1**

Note how you only see each transaction type listed once, but Author B is listed three times, once per transaction type.

For Values, the order just dictates which one will be displayed first in the table. Here I have Net Units Sold in the first position and Converted Currency in the second position:

	A	B	C
1			
2	Transaction Type (Multiple Items)	⍿	
3			
4	**Row Labels** ⍅	**Sum of Net Units Sold**	**Sum of Converted Currency**
5	Author A	1242	$6,415.27
6	Author B	19	$59.52
7	Author C	3	$8.98
8	Author D	80	$305.28
9	Author E	4	$17.55
10	Author G	1	$0.42
11	(blank)	1440	
12	**Grand Total**	**2789**	**$6,807.02**
13			

For Filters the order doesn't matter.

One final note here. Be very careful if you have multiple fields in more than one section of your pivot table. It can be done, but it can also get really messy really fast. Always ask yourself if what you've done is the best way to present this information. Maybe two tables is a better choice.

Expand/Collapse Fields

When you have more than one field in a column or row in a pivot table, you can expand and collapse the levels to show or hide the detail below. This can be done one entry at a time, or across all entries at once.

It's easy enough to hide or show the detail for one particular entry, you just click on the plus or minus sign to the left of the label. Plus expands, minus collapses (hides).

Here I've put Author Name on top and Marketplace underneath in the Rows section, and then clicked on the negative sign next to Author A to collapse that detail.

Sum of Net Units Sold	Column Labels								
	<12/10/2020	<12/10/2020 Total	2020	2020 Total	2021				2021 Total
Row Labels	<12/10/2020		Qtr4		Qtr1	Qtr2	Qtr3	Qtr4	
Author A			1	1	880	114	122	120	1236
Author B					17	3			20
Amazon.co.uk					10				10
Amazon.com					4	3			7
Amazon.com.au					3				3
Author C					90				90
Amazon.ca					3				3
Amazon.co.uk					1				1
Amazon.com					81				81
Amazon.de					3				3
Amazon.fr					1				1
Amazon.in					1				1
Author D			1	1	50	16	8	5	79
Amazon.co.uk					3				3
Amazon.com			1	1	46	16	8	5	75
Amazon.com.au					1				1

Author A now has a plus sign I can click if I want to expand that part of the table again. Authors B, C, and D still have a minus sign and show all of their related marketplace details.

To collapse or expand all entries for a specific level at once, right-click on one of the values (Author A, Author B, etc.), go to the Expand/Collapse option in the dropdown menu, and then use the secondary dropdown menu to make your choice.

For each level you have in a pivot table, the bottom of that dropdown will show an option to expand or collapse to that level:

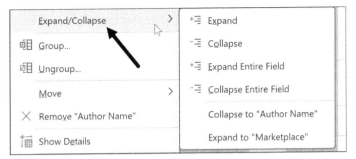

Expand Entire Field shows all of the detail for all values at that level in the table; Collapse Entire Field hides all the details for all values at that level.

Collapse and Expand just collapse or expand for that item at that level in the pivot table.

(I usually just end up playing around with the different choices when I need this rather than memorizing it.)

Remove a Field

The easiest way to remove a field that you were using to build your pivot table is to just uncheck the box next to its name in the PivotTable Fields task pane.

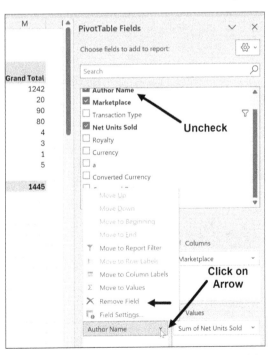

You can also left-click on the arrow next to the name of the field in the bottom section, and choose Remove from the dropdown menu.

This is the best approach if you were using that field more than once in the table (which we'll discuss later).

Another option is to right-click on a value in the pivot table itself, and then choose "Remove [Field Name]" from there.

If you were using that field as a filter, it is best to unfilter first before you remove the field, or the data in your table may remain filtered.

Move a Field

To move a field to a different section of your pivot table (Rows to Columns, Columns to Rows, Filters to Rows, etc.), you can left-click on the field name in the bottom section of the task pane and drag it to the section where you want it.

You can also left-click on the arrow for that field in the bottom section of the task pane to choose a new location from that dropdown menu.

Or you can right-click on the field name in the top of the task pane, and choose a location from that dropdown menu.

If you already had the field in a section, Excel will remove it from that prior section to place it in the new one.

(Also, note that Undo is a little tricky here. If you move a field, realize that was a mistake, and want to move it back, you will probably need to click into your worksheet first before Undo will work.)

Sort Results

You can sort the data in your pivot table. For example, I often want my largest values in my grand total column at the top.

To sort, right-click on a value in the column you want to sort by, go to the Sort option, and in the secondary dropdown menu choose the type of sort you want:

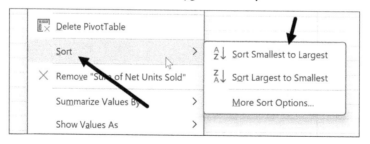

The nice thing about sorting in a pivot table is that all of your values stay together. You don't have to worry about breaking your data if you don't select the whole table first.

If you sort your column values, the sort will automatically be a left to right sort, but if you want a left to right sort for the calculated values in your table, you need to use More Sort Options in the Sort secondary dropdown. That will bring up the Sort by Value dialogue box, where you can then tell Excel you want a left to right sort:

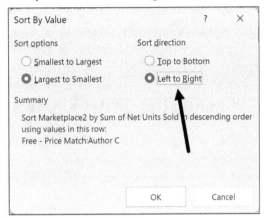

Move Column or Row Entries In the Pivot Table

You can also manually rearrange the column or row entries in your pivot table.

To do so, right-click on a value that you want to move, go down to the Move option, and then use the secondary dropdown menu to choose whether to move the value to the Beginning, the End, up one space, or down one space:

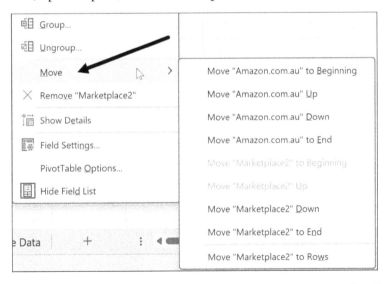

When working with values in the Columns section, think of Up as meaning "to the left" and Down as meaning "to the right".

It can help to think through the ultimate order you want your values in before you start doing this. For example, it's easier to move a field to the beginning and then down one, rather than move it up five times.

And sometimes you can save a lot of effort by moving your fields to the beginning or end in the order that puts the one you truly want at the end in that end position last.

We'll discuss a few more organizing your table options in the next chapter, but for now let's cover some more basics that you need to know.

Change Calculation Type

One of the issues I run into often with pivot tables and my data, is that Excel defaults to count when I drag my number fields into the Values section.

Fortunately, Excel will still sum those values if I ask it to, and it also does indicate what calculation it is performing on a field in the Value section of the PivotTable Fields task pane. (If you look above, you'll see that it was summing net units sold, for example.)

If you ever need to change the type of calculation, one option is to click on the dropdown arrow for that field in the Values section, and then choose Value Field Settings from the dropdown menu:

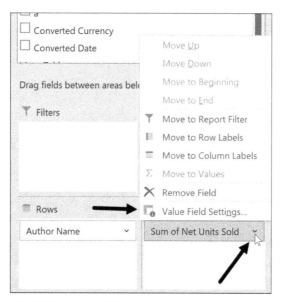

That will open the Value Field Settings dialogue box:

In the Summarize Value Field By section of the dialogue box, you will then see a list of the possible calculations that Excel can perform. It's the standard list of Sum, Count, Average, Max (maximum), Min (minimum), Product, Count Numbers, standard deviation, and variance that you will see throughout Excel. Just click on the option you want and then click OK. (I usually also format my cells at this point in time. We'll talk about that in a moment.)

When you change the calculation type, the Custom Name field will update accordingly.

Another way to choose the calculation type is to right-click on a calculated value in the pivot table itself, and then use the secondary dropdown menu for Summarize Values By:

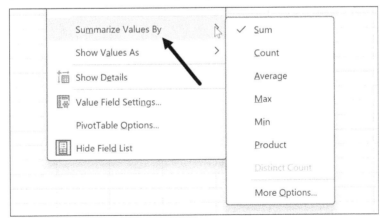

That approach doesn't require opening the dialogue box, so is pretty handy to use. It is a more limited list, but usually I just want Count or Sum, so it would work for me, I'm just used to the other way.

Excel also has a Show Values As option in that dropdown menu or as a tab in the Value Field Settings dialogue box:

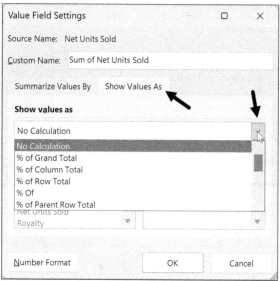

By default, that is going to show as No Calculation, which basically means it will display the result of the calculation you chose for Summarize Values By. (Sum, Count, etc.) But if you click on the dropdown arrow in the dialogue box, or use the secondary menu from the pivot table, you can choose to have Excel show your result as a percentage calculation, a difference from some value, a running total, a rank, or an index:

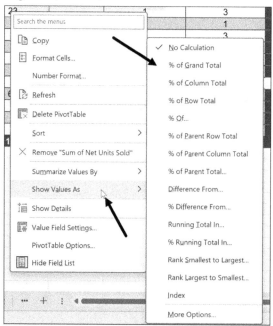

For example, I am sometimes not as interested in the number of units sold by an author in a marketplace as I am in what *percent* of sales that author represents in each marketplace. I have some marketplaces (the U.S.) with much larger absolute sales numbers, so sales in other markets (like France) look small in comparison no matter what. But it's valuable to know if Author A is 60% of sales in both of those markets or only one of them. That can help me make advertising decisions for each market.

The first step if you're going to do this, is to choose the correct calculation for Summarize Values By. (Sum or Count, usually.) After you do that, go to Show Values As, and pick the type of calculation you want displayed.

Here is that same data from our author and marketplace pivot table above, but now set to show the percentage of the column total instead of units:

	A	B	C	D	E	F	G	H
1								
2								
3								
4	Sum of Net Units Sold	Column Labels ▾						
5	Row Labels ▾	Amazon.ca	Amazon.co.uk	Amazon.com	Amazon.com.au	Amazon.com.mx	Amazon.de	Amazon.es
6	Author A	83.33%	85.71%	86.91%	42.86%	100.00%	0.00%	100.00%
7	Author B	0.00%	9.52%	0.54%	42.86%	0.00%	0.00%	0.00%
8	Author C	16.67%	0.95%	6.24%	0.00%	0.00%	100.00%	0.00%
9	Author D	0.00%	2.86%	5.85%	14.29%	0.00%	0.00%	0.00%
10	Author E	0.00%	0.00%	0.23%	0.00%	0.00%	0.00%	0.00%
11	Author F	0.00%	0.00%	0.23%	0.00%	0.00%	0.00%	0.00%
12	Author G	0.00%	0.95%	0.00%	0.00%	0.00%	0.00%	0.00%
13	(blank)	0.00%	0.00%	0.00%	0.00%	0.00%	0.00%	0.00%
14	Grand Total	100.00%	100.00%	100.00%	100.00%	100.00%	100.00%	100.00%

It's a little hard to read because of all of the 0.00% entries, but if you can wade through that, you can see that Author A tends to be the majority of sales in each marketplace, but is not in Australia (AU) and Germany (DE). That would be worth exploring more. (And we can fix that formatting to make this easier to read.)

Note that it is possible in the Values section to add the same field more than once. So you can, for example, show the sum or count value AND a % value.

Here, for example, I have actual number of units sold by author as well as the percent of the total:

	A	B	C
1			
2			
3	Row Labels ▾	Units Sold	Percent of Units Sold
4	Author C	90	6.25%
5	Author E	4	0.28%
6	Author B	20	1.39%
7	Author A	1242	86.25%
8	Author D	80	5.56%
9	Author F	3	0.21%
10	Author G	1	0.07%
11	(blank)		0.00%
12	Grand Total	1440	100.00%
13			

(I took out marketplace because it would have been way too busy and also renamed the columns to something friendlier and formatted them to center the values.)

A Caution

If you ever build a pivot table that has more than one different field in the Values section, be careful about using different calculations for each column. If you put a column that has a count of values next to another that has a sum of values next to another that has an average, it is possible someone will mistake the type of calculation being performed in one of those columns. You can do it, no one will stop you, just step back and ask yourself how someone who didn't build the table and is maybe in a hurry is going to interpret it. This is when changing your column labels will really be useful.

Rename a Field

Speaking of. You can rename a field that you're using in your pivot table by clicking on the cell that has the field name in it and then changing the name in the formula bar. If you try to use the original field name, though, you will get an error message that the name already exists. So if I want to rename "Sum of Net Units Sold" which was built using the "Net Units Sold" field, I can use "Units Sold", no problem, but I can't use "Net Units Sold" again.

You can also change the name by going to the Active Field section of the PivotTable Analyze tab, but that takes more effort.

Format Values

Another issue I almost always encounter with pivot tables is that the numbers won't be formatted the way I want them to be. For example, my currency values never seem to be formatted as currency by default.

You can technically just select the visible cells in the table, go to the Home tab, and use the formatting options there like you would with any other cell in Excel, but I do not recommend that. Because the formatting you apply to those cells will not carry through if the table updates.

The better way to format your values is to use the Value Field Settings dialogue box. (Right click on the field name in the Values section and choose Value Field Settings from the dropdown to open it.)

From the dialogue box, click on the bottom left corner where it says Number Format. That will bring up the Format Cells dialogue box, where you can then choose the number format you want applied to that field. Click OK to close the Format Cells dialogue box, and then OK to close the Value Field Settings dialogue box when you're done.

Here, for example, I've changed the formatting of the percentage values to not have two decimal places, which makes it a little easier to read:

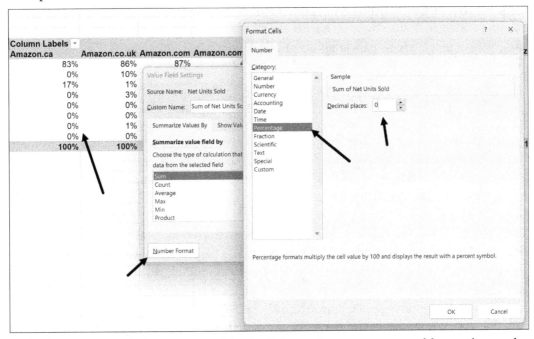

(I made the change and then reopened both dialogue boxes so you could see what each one looks like.)

Refresh Pivot Table

Your pivot table will not automatically recalculate everything when you add new data to the original data source. To update your table, go to the Data section of the PivotTable Analyze tab, and you'll see Refresh:

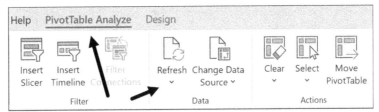

Click on the image there and your table should update to show your changes.

You can also choose Refresh All from the dropdown there, and that will update all pivot tables in the workbook.

There are control shortcuts for this, too, but I never use them. They are Alt + F5 and Ctrl + Alt + F5, respectively.

(One thing to be careful of with Refresh is that it can undo some of your custom formatting, so try to finalize your data before you get fancy with the formatting. Microsoft support seems to think that the PivotTable Options choices can fix this, but it didn't for me when I just tried it. Honestly, I normally don't need pretty formatting of my pivot tables because they're just there for my analysis and I take the results elsewhere if I need them for a report.)

Change Data Source

There are going to be times when you need to change the data that Excel is using for a pivot table. Maybe you add a new column of data that you want to use, or you were selecting a cell range for the table and have now added more rows of data that you need to capture. When that happens, you can go to the Data section of the PivotTable Analyze tab, and click on Change Data Source.

That will take you to the worksheet where the data is, and also bring up the Change PivotTable Data Source dialogue box. The easiest way, in my opinion, to change the data source is to just left-click and drag in the worksheet to select the full range of cells to use in the pivot table. That should update the cell range in the dialogue box and you can then just click on OK to close it. Your pivot table should automatically update based on your new cell range.

Another option is to click into the field in the dialogue box and manually adjust the range of cells being referenced. I do this when I add another column of data because I can just click at the end, backspace out the last listed column letter, and type in the new letter.

Just be careful with this approach, because using arrows to move within the text in that input field does not work well. (It will start populating a cell range for you in the midst of the one you already had.) If you go with this approach and are making significant changes, I think it's best to delete out what's there first, and then you can hold down Shift as you arrow around to select the new cell range.

If you don't want to do that, then click exactly where you need to make your edit in that field, and use backspace or delete before type in your values from there.

Just do not use the arrow keys.

A Quick Caution

One final note here about refresh, change data sources, and filtering. I've noticed lately that Excel is a little less stable when using these than it used to be. It sometimes doesn't update the values. So be sure to "gut check" that your table results look right. Maybe make sure the grand total is what you expect, or that all the values you should be seeing are there.

Do something to independently confirm your results if you're using refresh, change data sources, or filters.

There have been a couple times in Excel 365, where I have had to do a brand new pivot table to get it to work properly. Also, when I was playing around here with two fields in the Filter section and then removed them, one of the filters continued to apply to my table even though I'd supposedly taken it away. That's why I suggested unfiltering your table first.

Pivot tables are great and invaluable, so don't let that scare you away from using them. Just understand that for anything you do in Excel, you should always make sure the result makes sense.

Clear Your Pivot Table

If you ever build a pivot table and want to just start over from scratch, you can go to the Actions section of the PivotTable Analyze tab and choose Clear.

If you have filters in place on your table, you can use Clear Filters from the dropdown menu to reset those.

Pivot Tables – More Advanced Topics

The last chapter covered the basics of building a pivot table and editing it a bit. I'd say I can get away with only the information in that chapter for probably 90%-95% of what I do with pivot tables. (There are a few more items in the formatting chapter that I use regularly.) But there are a lot of bells and whistles with pivot tables, and they're adding more functionality all the time, so let's walk through some of those more advanced topics now.

Working with Dates

In more recent version of Excel, pivot tables have gotten really useful for working with dates. But only if Excel recognizes the field as a date field. Given Excel's tendency to turn anything remotely close to a date into a date, it is kind of ironic how difficult it can be sometimes to get Excel to treat an actual date as a date for pivot table purposes. (I put some tips at the start of this book, but sometimes even those don't work.)

Okay. So what can Excel do with dates?

When you add a date field to the Rows or Columns section of a pivot table, Excel will create up to four separate date fields for you in that section. You'll have the actual date field, but Excel will also create fields for year, quarter, and month based on your date values. (Assuming your dates span multiple months, quarters, and/or years.)

Here I dragged Royalty Date to the Columns section and you can see the new fields Excel created for me.

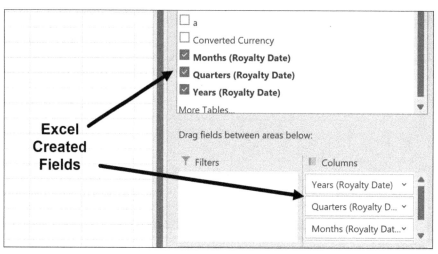

This is either going to be very useful to you or very annoying, depending on what you were trying to do.

I find it very useful, because usually I am not concerned that X event happened on a specific date; I am more interested that it happened in 2022 or in January of 2022. Which means I really like that Excel breaks my date data down for me automatically. Then I can just uncheck the fields it created that I don't want to use.

Once Excel creates those options for you, they'll still be listed as available fields that you can add to your table at any time.

Now, I mentioned in the quick tips section that when I wrote the first draft of this book I was able to get Excel to work with my date column no problem with that convert text to columns trick, but then it stopped working and nothing I did could get Excel to treat that column of values as a date for a pivot table.

I could see that the number for that cell was a date value. I could use it in math. But Excel treated each date as a unique value for my pivot table. (I eventually did a full repair on my version of Office, something I've never had to do before.)

Good news is that dealing with that led me to discover another option for displaying your dates by month, quarter, and year that I hadn't known before. (I do not in fact know everything. I am very lazy. I learn what I need and do it that way until I get stuck and need to learn a new way. Anyway.)

If Excel doesn't automatically create month, quarter, and year versions of your date values for you, but the entries are formatted as dates, right-click on one of the values in your table, and choose Group. That will bring up a Grouping dialogue box:

You can choose from there months, quarters, or years. (Days, hours, minutes, or seconds, too.) Click on the one you need, and then OK, and it will break your data down by those categories.

Now, be careful with this. Because I had dates as text and it let me do it but then showed the date values as 1905 dates. So you still need to go through all the steps to turn your date into a date entry in the data table first. But it seems to work even when Excel is being weird.

Insert Timeline

Insert Timeline creates a dialogue box that you can use to filter your pivot table in real-time based on a date field. It is also more visible than filtering. You can always see exactly which date criteria are being applied to a table.

To create a timeline, go to the Filter section of the PivotTable Analyze tab, and click on Insert Timeline. That will bring up the Insert Timelines dialogue box:

Timelines are only available for fields that Excel thinks are dates for pivot table purposes. So when you click on that option, the only fields that will show are those fields.

Click the checkbox for the one that you want, and then click OK.

Excel will then create a timeline dialogue box for that specific field that you can use to filter your pivot table:

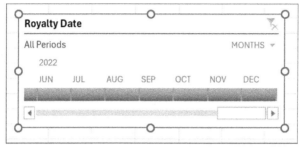

The range of values in the dialogue box will cover the entire date range of values for that field, even if some days, months, quarters, or years in the midst of the range have no data related with them. If you select days, months, quarters, or years that have no results, the pivot table will be blank.

There is a dropdown in the top right corner of the timeline that you can change to different time periods. If your dates cover it, you should be able to choose years, quarters, months, or days. After you do that, just click on the timeline to choose a specific value or range of values.

So I can do MONTHS, and then click on Jul for a specific year, and have only results for July of that year show in my pivot table.

If you want to select a range of months, days, years, etc., click on the starting value you want and hold down the Shift key while you click on the last value in you want.

Here, for example, I've selected January to March 2021:

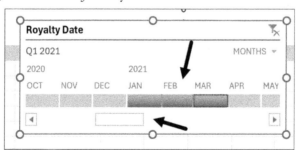

It is not possible to select non-contiguous dates. So you can't select June and October 2021, you have to select June *through* October.

There is a white outlined scroll bar below the date values that you can use to move through the entire range of available dates on the timeline.

To remove your timeline filter from your pivot table, just click on the funnel with an X in the top right corner of the dialogue box.

Right-click on the dialogue box and choose Remove Timeline to get rid of it. Your data may remain filtered if you were also using that field to build the table.

Insert Slicer

Insert Slicer lets you have a visible filter for all of your non-date fields. It can also be found in the Filter section of the PivotTable Analyze tab. Click on Insert Slicer, and then check the box for the field(s) you want to have a slicer for. Click OK when you're done.

Excel will insert slicers for each selected field. The slicers show all possible values for that field. Here, for example, are filters for net units sold and transaction type:

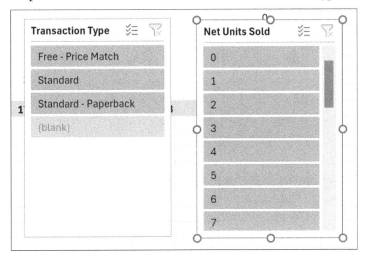

Click on a value to filter the pivot table by that value. Hold down the Ctrl key to select more than one value at once or the Shift key to select a range of values.

The multiselect option, at the top, next to the funnel, will let you choose more than one value without having to hold down the Ctrl key.

Turn off the filter by clicking on the funnel with an X in the top right corner.

Close the slicer by right-clicking and choosing the Remove option.

Grouping Row or Column Values

You can also manually group values in the rows or columns sections.

For example, in this data set I have three transaction categories: Free – Price Match, Standard, and Standard – Paperback. If I want to combine Standard and Standard-Paperback into one entry, I can do that.

To group values together, click on the first value you want in your group, and then hold down Ctrl and click on the other values you want to include.

Right-click when you have them all selected, and choose Group from the dropdown menu. (Or you can choose Group Selection from the Group section of the PivotTable Analyze tab.)

By default, Excel will give that new grouping the name Group1.

It will also assign all remaining values for that field to their own group with a group name that is identical to the value. For example, you can see here that I have a Group 1 that contains my two standard transaction types, as well as a group named (blank) that contains (blank) and one named Free – Price Match that contains Free – Price Match:

	A	B
1		
2	Author Name	(All)
3		
4	**Row Labels**	**Sum of Net Unit**
5	**Free - Price Match**	
6	Free - Price Match	
7	**(blank)**	
8	(blank)	
9	**Group1**	
10	Standard	
11	Standard - Paperback	
12	**Grand Total**	

If you create more than one group for values in a field, Excel will just keep naming the groups with the next available number, so Group 2, Group 3, etc.

To change the name of a group, click on the name in the pivot table, go to the formula bar, and change the text in the formula bar to the name you want.

Here I'm clicked onto Cell A9 and have changed the name to Standard Transactions:

A9	f_x	Standard Transactions	
	A		
1			
2	Author Name	(All)	
3			
4	**Row Labels**	**Sum of Net Units Sold**	**Sum o**
5	**Free - Price Match**		
6	Free - Price Match	91	
7	**(blank)**		
8	(blank)	1440	
9	**Standard Transactions**		
10	Standard	306	
11	Standard - Paperback	1043	

To add to an existing group, you need to select the fields that are already members of that group and then select the new values you want to include. So in the example above, I'd need to select Standard and Standard – Paperback, and then click on the field that was missing at that same level, and choose Group again..

To ungroup values, right-click on the group name, and choose Ungroup from the dropdown menu. Or click on the group name and then choose Ungroup from the Group section of the PivotTable Analyze tab.

See Underlying Data

If you ever need to see the specific entries from your original data table that led to a value in your pivot table, either double-click on that value, or right-click and choose Show Details.

Excel will create a new worksheet that has a data table showing all of the specific rows of data that led to that value:

	A	B	C	D	E	F	G	H	I
1	Royalty Date	Author Name	Marketplace	Transaction Type	Net Units Sold	Royalty	Currency	a	Converted Currency
2	2/1/2021	Author A	Amazon.co.uk	Standard	1	1.64	GBP		1.98
3	2/1/2021	Author A	Amazon.co.uk	Standard	1	1.64	GBP		1.98
4	2/1/2021	Author A	Amazon.co.uk	Standard	1	1.62	GBP		1.96
5	2/1/2021	Author A	Amazon.co.uk	Standard	1	1.67	GBP		2.02
6	2/1/2021	Author A	Amazon.co.uk	Standard	1	1.72	GBP		2.08
7	3/1/2021	Author A	Amazon.co.uk	Standard	0	0	GBP		0
8	6/1/2021	Author A	Amazon.co.uk	Standard	1	3.61	GBP		4.37
9	6/1/2021	Author A	Amazon.co.uk	Standard	1	2.13	GBP		2.58
10	7/1/2021	Author A	Amazon.co.uk	Standard	1	2.04	GBP		2.47

Be careful with this one, though, because when I was just playing with it, it did not adjust when I changed my entries in the original data table and tried to Refresh. There was no connection between the two anymore. This could be due to my security settings, or whatever was impacting Excel's ability to recognize my dates, but it's something to watch out for.

I think for my purposes, I would generate the detail, review it as needed, and then delete that worksheet immediately. If I need it again, it's just one click to create it.

Recommended Pivot Tables

In the Tools section of the PivotTable Analyze tab, there is an option for Recommended PivotTables. It takes your data and suggests some possible pivot tables to build with it. If you see something you like, just click on the one you want and then OK.

Personally, I don't use it because it doesn't save me time, but if you ever forget how to build a pivot table or aren't sure how to approach your data, it could be a good starting point.

Calculations

If you want to create a calculation within a pivot table, it is possible. To do so, go to the Calculations section of the PivotTable Analyze tab, and click on the dropdown arrow for Fields, Items & Sets, and choose Calculated Field.

You can then build a formula in the dialogue box that opens using the field names as your inputs

I rarely if ever use this and am going to assign it to an advanced use of Excel rather than walk you through it here. I just wanted you to know it exists if you ever think you need it. For me, personally, if I want to do more with my pivot table data, I copy and paste special-values and then go from there. The only reason I'd do calculations in a pivot table was if I expected to use that pivot table with data that was going to update periodically and that's just not something I've ever needed in 30 years of doing some pretty intensive data analysis in Excel.

Pivot Tables – Formatting

I do format my pivot tables in Excel, especially if I'm going to copy and paste that data for further use elsewhere. The two biggest changes I make are to remove subtotals and grand totals and to change my report layout to make the pivot table a data table.

Subtotals and Grand Totals

The default when you have multiple fields in rows or columns is for Excel to insert subtotals for you. Which is great if you're treating your pivot table as some sort of report. But I am often trying to get data I can then work with elsewhere, so I don't want those subtotals. It clutters things up, gets in the way, and I'd just want to delete them later,.

To remove any subtotals or grand totals used in your pivot table, go to the Layout section of the Design tab. You will see two dropdowns, Subtotals and Grand Totals. Here is the dropdown for Subtotals:

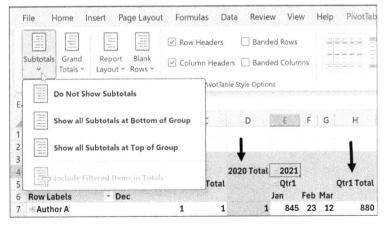

Click on the dropdown arrow for each one and select the option you want.

As you can see, for subtotals there are options for where your subtotals appear, "top" or "bottom". That means before the detail or after it. The default is top but sometimes I prefer it to be on the bottom.

Report Layout

To change how your data displays in your pivot table, go to the Layout section of the Design tab, and click on the Report Layout dropdown menu:

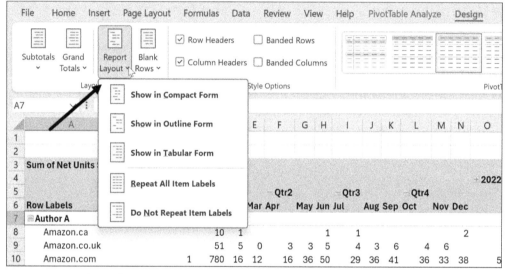

There are two sections there.

The top lets you decide if you want your pivot table rows to be Compact, which is the default, Outline format, or Tabular format. You can sort of see what the layout will look like in those little thumbnails, but I usually end up applying each one to find the one I want.

The second section lets you decide about repeating values for your columns.

By default, Excel does not repeat item labels. You can see below that 2021 shows once in Row 4, but not above each quarter and month that is part of 2021. Same with Qtr1 of 2021. Qtr1 shows once in Row 5 above Jan, but not above Feb and March. Fine for a report, but not for a data table that requires more analysis.

3	Sum of Net Units Sold	Column Labels														
4			2020	2021												2022
5			Qtr4	Qtr1			Qtr2			Qtr3			Qtr4			
6	Row Labels		Dec	Jan	Feb	Mar	Apr	May	Jun	Jul	Aug	Sep	Oct	Nov	Dec	
7	Author A		1	845	23	12	19	39	56	35	40	47	40	40	40	5
8	Author B			17			2	1								
9	Author C			90												
10	Author D		1	47		3	4	2	10	1	5	2	2	3		

To reformat a pivot table for data analysis I change the settings to Tabular form, Repeat Item Labels, no subtotals, and no grand totals. That gives me this:

	A	B	C	D	E
1					
2					
3	Sum of Net Units Sold		Years (Royalty Date) .⊤	Quarters (Royalty Date) ▾	Months (Royalty Date) ▾
4			2020	2021	2021
5			Qtr4	Qtr1	Qtr1
6	Author Name ▾	Marketplace ▾	Dec	Jan	Feb
7	Author A	Amazon.ca		10	1
8	Author A	Amazon.co.uk		51	5
9	Author A	Amazon.com	1	780	16
10	Author A	Amazon.com.au		2	
11	Author A	Amazon.com.mx			1
12	Author A	Amazon.es			
13	Author A	Amazon.fr			

Much better. I can now copy this worksheet and paste special – values into another worksheet, and have all of my rows and columns fully complete so I can do more analysis.

Other Formatting

Most of your pivot table formatting options will be in the Design tab. We already talked about the options on the left-hand side that cover subtotals, grand totals, and report layout. Now let's cover the rest:

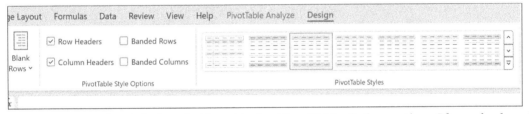

I want to start on the right-hand side with the PivotTable Styles section. If you look really close, you may be able to see that there is a box around the third option displayed there. That's because that is the current style that is by default being applied to my pivot table.

It has a color across the top row and the grand totals row at the bottom. When there are two fields used for rows, it also puts a light blue line between different values for the top-level field. (Not a row, a line.)

All but the first option in that first row are just different colored versions of that format. The first option uses a colored row to separate the different values when there are two levels in the row section.

If you look at the right-hand side there, you should see an up and a down arrow as well as a down arrow with a line behind it. Click on that arrow with the line behind it to see more formatting choices:

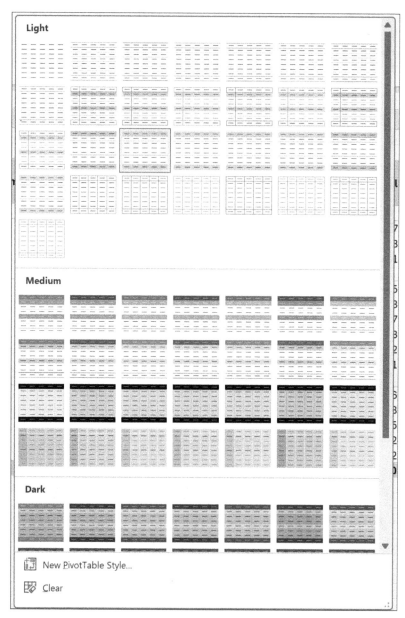

Hold your mouse over each one to see how it will look with your data (like I have on the next page).

If you like an option, click on it to apply.

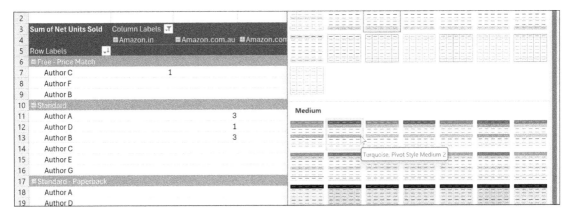

You should choose a style based upon the nature of the pivot table you created.

For example, some of the styles have a different format for the bottom row. Great if you have grand totals in your final row, but weird if you don't.

Same with the final column of the table. Some styles have a different format, which is great if you have a grand total column, but you shouldn't use it if you don't.

As you can see here, while I like this style and its color choices, the formatting isn't working with my data, because I do have a grand total column but this format doesn't treat that last column differently:

	A	B	C	D	E	F	G	H	I
1									
2									
3	Sum of Net Units Sold	Column Labels							
4		🔲Amazon.in	🔲Amazon.com.au	🔲Amazon.com.mx	🔲Amazon.com	🔲Amazon.co.uk	🔲Amazon.ca	🔲Amazon Europe	Grand Total
5	Row Labels								
6	🔲Free - Price Match								
7	Author C	1			78	1	3	4	87
8	Author F				3				3
9	Author B				1				1
10	🔲Standard								
11	Author A		3	1	218	23	7	3	255
12	Author D		1		26	1			28
13	Author B		3		5	9			17
14	Author C				3				3
15	Author E				1			1	2
16	Author G					1			1
17	🔲Standard - Paperback								
18	Author A				905	63	7	1	976
19	Author D				46	2			48
20	Author Z				5				5
21	Author B				1	1			2
22	Author E				2				2
23	Grand Total	1	7	1	1294	101	17	9	1430

I could try to find another style that works better. (You basically go down the column to find the varying styles and then across to find different color schemes.)

Or, I could start with this, and then customize it using the Font section of the Home tab.

In the table on the next page I bolded the last column, added fill color to the bottom row, changed my font color, and added a line to separate my left-most column and my right-most column. I also centered all of the numbers, and hid Rows 3 and 5:

	Amazon.in	Amazon.com.au	Amazon.com.mx	Amazon.com	Amazon.co.uk	Amazon.ca	Amazon Europe	Grand Total
Free - Price Match								
Author C	1			78	1	3	4	87
Author F				3				3
Author B				1				1
Standard								
Author A		3	1	218	23	7	3	255
Author D		1		26	1			28
Author B		3		5	9			17
Author C				3				3
Author E				1			1	2
Author G					1			1
Standard - Paperback								
Author A				911	67	8	1	987
Author D				50	2			52
Author E				2				2
Author B				1	1			2
Grand Total	1	7	1	1299	105	18	9	1440

Not bad. But you have to be careful when you depart from an existing pivot table style, because if you then change your data or refresh the table, you can lose some of that formatting. Not all, weirdly enough, but some.

So preferably save your formatting for last.

Custom Style

It is possible to create a customized pivot table style by going to the very bottom of the PivotTable Styles dropdown and clicking on New PivotTable Style.

That will bring up a dialogue box where you can fully customize the table appearance and save that customized look for use with the current table or any others in the workbook. If you're going to routinely update your data that feeds the pivot table and you don't like any of the default styles, you should either go with a default style or create a custom one.

If you choose to customize, in the dialogue box click on the name of each table element in the list, and then click on Format to bring up a Format Cells dialogue box, which will allow you to control any font attributes, borders, and fill colors. Make your choices, click OK, and then move on to the next element.

The Preview in the main dialogue box should show you what your table will look like with all of the elements formatted according to your choices.

If there is a style that already is partially what you want, right-click on it and choose Duplicate from the dropdown menu. That will start you with a style that already has all of that formatting applied, and you can then make additional changes from there.

When you're done, if you want all new pivot tables to automatically use the style you created, click on the Set As Default box at the bottom before you click OK.

* * *

Three more formatting options to discuss form the Design tab:

Blank Rows

The Blank Rows option in the Layout section of the Design tab lets you add blank rows between each grouped item in your rows. For a table like the one above it really doesn't do much, but if I take that same table and add a subtotal for each top-level category, then it does help a bit with visual separation:

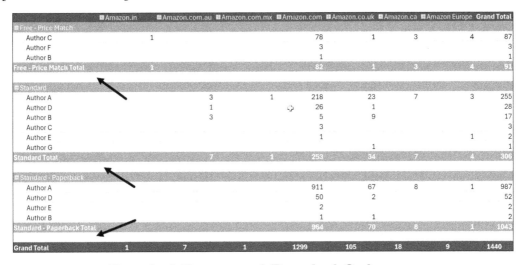

	Amazon.in	Amazon.com.au	Amazon.com.mx	Amazon.com	Amazon.co.uk	Amazon.ca	Amazon Europe	Grand Total
Free - Price Match								
Author C	1			78	1	3	4	87
Author F				3				3
Author B				1				1
Free - Price Match Total	1			82	1	3	4	91
Standard								
Author A		3	1	218	23	7	3	255
Author D		1		26	1			28
Author B		3		5	9			17
Author C				3				3
Author E				1			1	2
Author G					1			1
Standard Total		7	1	253	34	7	4	306
Standard - Paperback								
Author A				911	67	8	1	987
Author D				50	2			52
Author E				2				2
Author B				1	1			2
Standard - Paperback Total				964	70	8	1	1043
Grand Total	1	7	1	1299	105	18	9	1440

Banded Rows and Banded Columns

You can add banded rows or banded columns to any pivot table from the PivotTable Style Options section of the Design tab. Banded just means that every other column or row will be a different color. For example, here is banded columns:

4		Amazon.in	Amazon.com.au	Amazon.com.mx
6	Free - Price Match			
7	Author C	1		
8	Author F			
9	Author B			

See how every other column is a different color?

Here is banded rows:

4		Amazon.in	Amazon.com.au	Amazon.com.mx
6	Free - Price Match			
7	Author C	1		
8	Author F			
9	Author B			

The appearance of banded rows or columns is going to vary depending on the PivotTable Style you're using. For this style, for example, clicking both banded rows and columns just added a nice little line around each cell:

4		▦ Amazon.in	▦ Amazon.com.au	▦ Amazon.com.mx	▦ Amazon.com
6	▣ Free - Price Match				
7	Author C	1			78
8	Author F				3
9	Author B				1

But for other styles it has a much bigger impact and I wouldn't recommend using both at the same time.

When choosing which one to use, if you think your data will primarily be read left to right, then banded rows can create good visual separation that makes that easier to do. If you think your data will primarily be read top to bottom, then banded columns will help.

Row and Column Header Formatting

There are also checkboxes in the PivotTable Style Options section of the Design tab for row headers or column headers. What unchecking those boxes does will depend on the style you chose. I recommend just clicking on them to see what you get.

Appendix A: Basic Terminology

Workbook

A workbook is what Excel likes to call an Excel file.

Worksheet

Excel defines a worksheet as the primary document you use in Excel to store and work with your data. A worksheet is organized into Columns and Rows that form Cells. A workbook can contain multiple worksheets.

Columns

Excel uses columns and rows to display information. Columns run across the top of the worksheet and, unless you've done something funky with your settings, are identified using letters of the alphabet.

The first column in a worksheet will always be Column A. And the number of columns in your worksheet will remain the same, regardless of how many columns you delete, add, or move around. Think of columns as location information that is actually separate from the data in the worksheet.

Rows

Rows run down the side of each worksheet and are numbered starting at 1 and up to a very high number. Row numbers are also locational information. The first row will always be numbered 1, the second row will always be numbered 2, and so on and so forth. There will also always be a fixed number of rows in each worksheet regardless of how many rows of data you delete, add, or move around.

Cells

Cells are where the row and column data comes together. Cells are identified using the letter for the column and the number for the row that intersect to form that cell. For example, Cell A1 is the cell that is in the first column and first row of the worksheet.

Click

If I tell you to click on something, that means to use your mouse (or trackpad) to move the cursor on the screen over to a specific location and left-click or right-click on the option. If you left-click, this selects the item. If you right-click, this generally displays a dropdown list of options to choose from. If I don't tell you which to do, left- or right-click, then left-click.

Left-click/Right-click

If you look at your mouse you generally have two flat buttons to press. One is on the left side, one is on the right. If I say left-click that means to press down on the button on the left. If I say right-click that means press down on the button on the right.

Select

If I tell you to "select" cells, that means to highlight them. You can either left-click and drag to select a range of cells or hold down the Ctrl key as you click on individual cells. To select an entire column, click on the letter for the column. To select an entire row, click on the number for the row.

Data

Data is the information you enter into your worksheet.

Data Table

I may also sometimes refer to a data table or table of data. This is just a combination of cells that contain data in them.

Arrow

If I tell you to arrow to somewhere or to arrow right, left, up, or down, this just means use the arrow keys to navigate to a new cell.

Cursor Functions

The cursor is what moves around when you move your mouse or use the trackpad. In Excel the cursor changes its appearance depending on what functions you can perform.

Tab

I am going to talk a lot about Tabs, which are the options you have to choose from at the top of the workspace. The default tab names are File, Home, Insert, Page Layout, Formulas, Data, Review, View, and Help. But there are certain times when additional tabs will appear, for example, when you create a pivot table or a chart.

(This should not be confused with the Tab key which can be used to move across cells.)

Dropdown Menus

A dropdown menu is a listing of available choices that you can see when you right-click in certain places such as the main workspace or on a worksheet name. You will also see them when you click on an arrow next to or below an option in the top menu.

Dialogue Boxes

Dialogue boxes are pop-up boxes that contain additional choices.

Scroll Bars

When you have more information than will show in a screen, dialogue box, or dropdown menu, you will see scroll bars on the right side or bottom that allow you to navigate to see the rest of the information.

Formula Bar

The formula bar is the long white bar at the top of the main workspace directly below the top menu options that lets you see the actual contents of a cell, not just the displayed value.

Cell Notation

Cells are referred to by their column and row position. So Cell A1 is the cell that's the intersection of the first column and first row in the worksheet.

When written in Excel you just use A1, you do not need to include the word cell. A colon (:) can be used to reference a range of cells. A comma (,) can be used to separate cell references.

When in doubt about how to define a cell range, click into a cell, type =, and then go and select the cells you want to reference. Excel will describe your selection in the formula bar using cell notation.

Paste Special Values

Paste Special Values is a way of pasting copied values that keeps the calculation results or the cell values but removes any formulas or formatting.

Task Pane

On occasion Excel will open a task pane, which is different from a dialogue box because it is part of the workspace. These will normally appear on the right-hand side in Excel for tasks such as working with pivot tables or charts or using the built-in Help function. (They often appear on the left-hand side in Word.)

They can be closed by clicking on the X in the top right corner.

About the Author

M.L. Humphrey is a former stockbroker with a degree in Economics from Stanford and an MBA from Wharton who has spent close to twenty years as a regulator and consultant in the financial services industry.

You can reach M.L. at mlhumphreywriter@gmail.com or at mlhumphrey.com.

* * *

If you want to learn more about Microsoft Excel, check out *Excel Tips and Tricks* or one of the main Excel 2024 Essentials titles, *Excel 2024 for Beginners*, *Intermediate Excel 2024*, or *Excel 2024 Useful Functions*.